D0819812

Where are the Rolling Stones?

Can you find the bad boys of rock 'n' roll?

igloobooks

Where are the Rolling Stones ?

Can you find the bad boys of rock 'n' roll?

Bands don't get much more rock 'n' roll than the Rolling Stones. Mick Jagger and the boys have jammed relentlessly through every decade since their formation in the 1960s and show no signs of stopping anytime soon. Along the way there have been shiny awards, worldwide tours, and epic parties. On the down side, there have been drink and drug problems, high-profile divorces, and near-death experiences. Given the nonstop whirlwind that comes with being a Stone, no one would judge them for craving the odd personal moment, if only to pop on some slippers and sip a restorative cup of tea.

All of the above begs the following question: where would the Stones have gone over the years for a bit of peace and quiet? Whether it's skulking about the set of *The Ed Sullivan Show* or getting lost among the heaving crowds at their free concert at Copacabana Beach, it's your mission to find out in this book!

There wouldn't have been much in the way of silence at The Ealing Jazz Club, which was one of Keith Richards's top nights out. The Stones eventually took to the stage here, too. By that time, they would have known every nook and cranny. Can you see the group among the cool cats and jazzy haze?

Another early haunt? The Crawdaddy Club, where the boys accepted a residency at the beginning of their career. With fans packed in like sardines, the Stones would have needed to get pretty creative with seeking out hideouts. Can you see them?

You might think that the Stones would have had some peace at home, but Villa Nellcôte, Keith's house on the French Riviera, was more party palace than sleepy sanctuary. The guitarist wasn't short on company during his time there, with even John Lennon supposedly stopping by. But never mind The Beatles. Can you see the Stones?

Or perhaps the Caribbean catches your fancy? It was the destination of choice in the early '70s, when the band exiled themselves to Jamaica to record their album *Goats Head Soup*. On the rare hours stolen away from the sound booths and mixing desks, Mick and the boys immersed themselves in some underwater downtime at the Terra Nova Hotel. Yet where are they making a (discreet) splash?

Back in Britain, Mick's Stargroves mansion in Hampshire was an even less likely place to escape the madness. Bob Marley, The Who, and Status Quo all reportedly recorded at the on-site mobile studio, but can you shine a light on any of the Stones?

As the Stones's musical horizons have expanded, so has their world. Far-flung destinations such as Fiji are just a hop, skip, and a jump away when you're on an international tour. And sometimes all that hopping, skipping, and jumping results in Keith falling out of a palm tree. Can you see him? Clue: he's not up the tree.

It's time to begin. Find your Jagger swagger, clean those sticky fingers, and open your eyes to spot not just the Stones, but also themed items and celebrity pals. It's dirty work going undercover, but if you try sometimes, you just might find… all of the Rolling Stones.

Mick Jagger   Ronnie Wood   Charlie Watts   Keith Richards

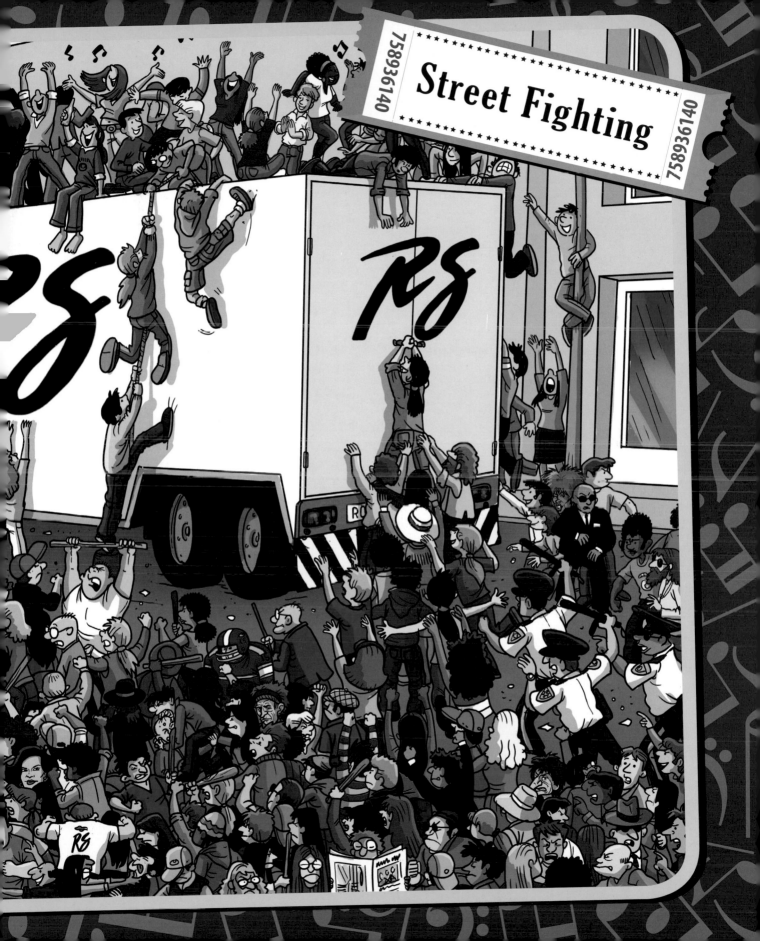

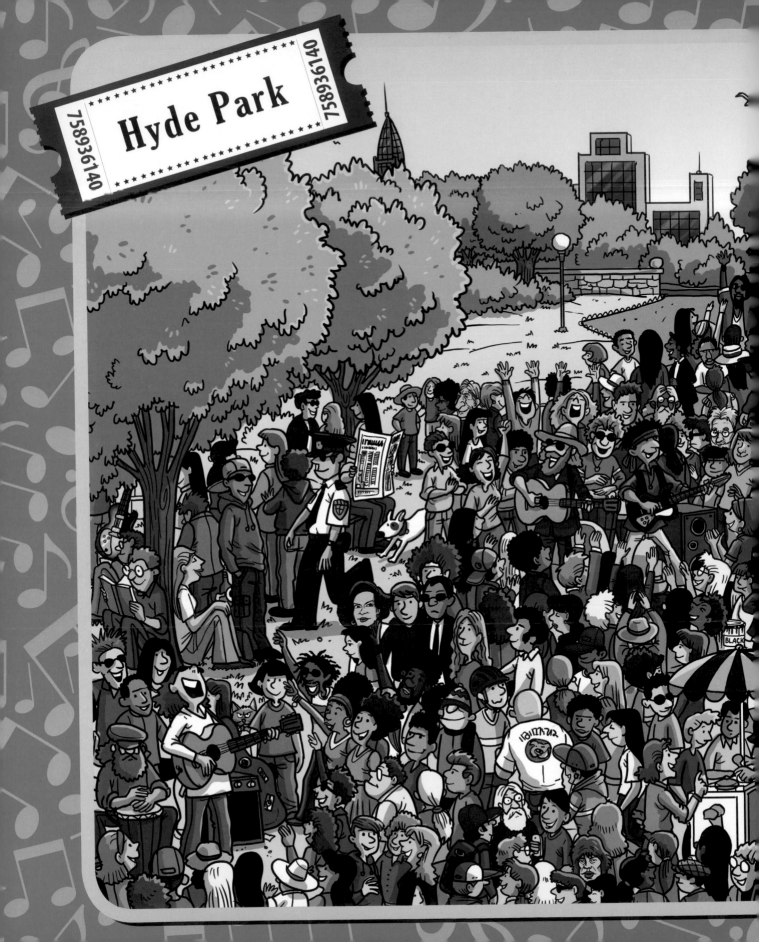

Stargroves

758936140
758936140

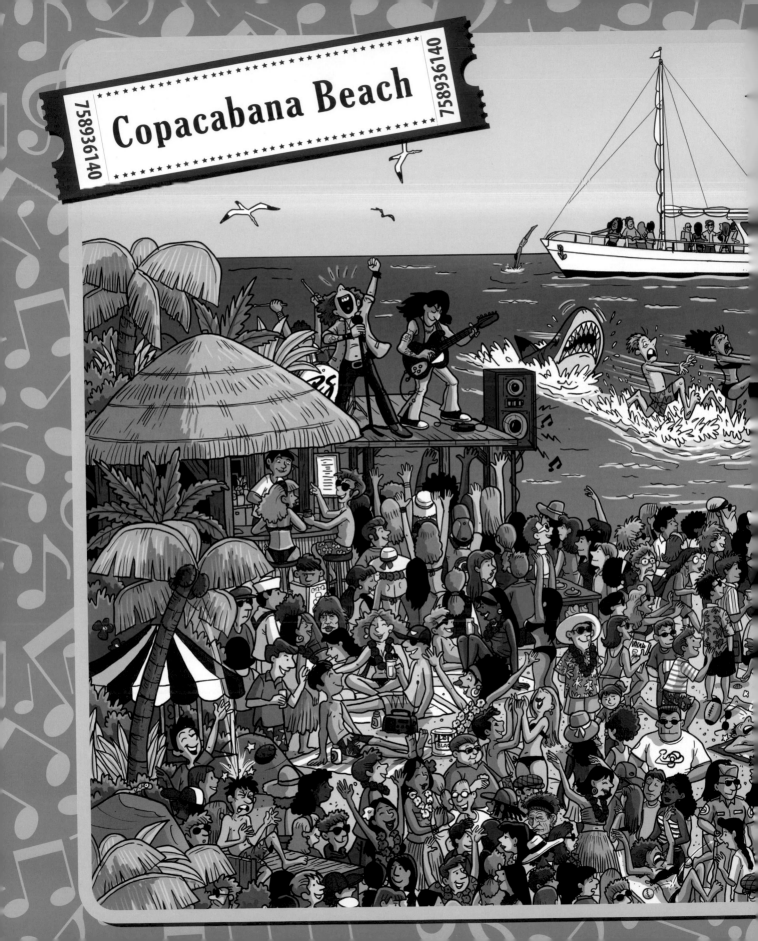

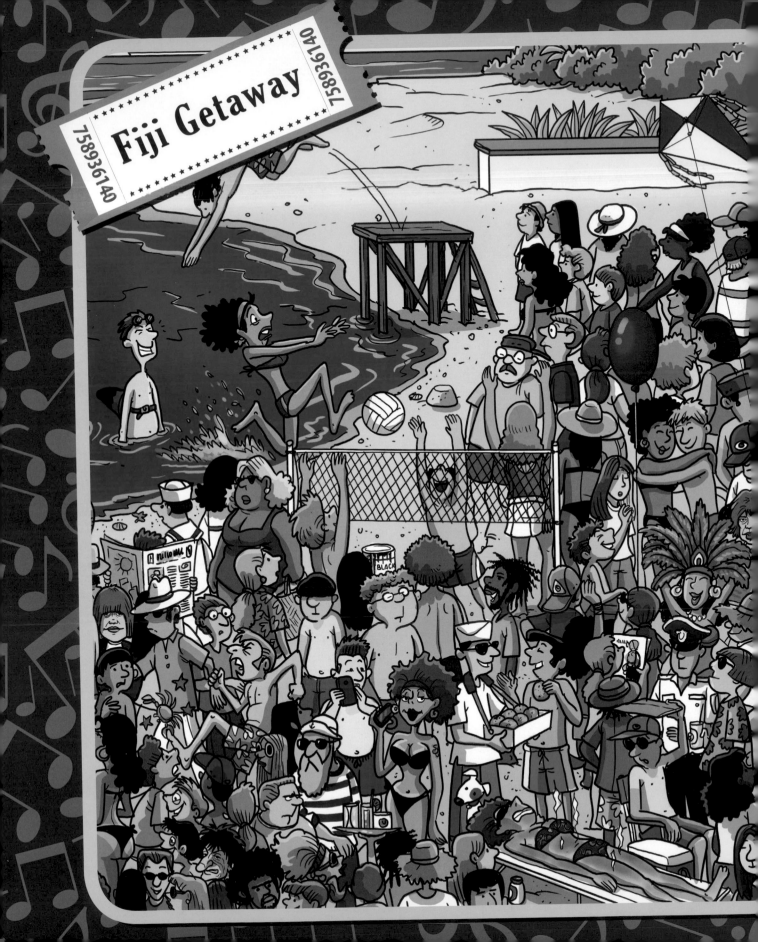

Did you also spot...?

758936140   758936140

Andrew Loog Oldham —
Oldham managed the band and
masterminded their bad-boy image.
The (somewhat obscene) song
"Andrew's Blues" was written about him.

Bianca Jagger —
A jet-setting actress and Studio 54 regular,
Bianca became Mick's first wife in 1971.
Her chic wedding suit remains a
style classic.

Bill Wyman —
The Stones's bass guitarist from 1962–
1993, Bill's collection of Rolling Stones
memorabilia is on display in his Sticky
Fingers restaurant.

Brian Jones —
A founding member of the Rolling Stones,
often credited with naming the band.
He left in 1969 and tragically died
months later, at the age of just 27.

Ian Stewart —
The so-called sixth Stone, Ian was the
band's pianist of choice until his death at
age 47 in 1985.

Jerry Hall —
Mick's American model wife, except their
1990 wedding wasn't actually legal.
They split in 1999.

Jo Wood —
Model Jo met Ronnie in 1977. The couple
was together for over 30 years, during
which time Jo worked as Ronnie's PA
and stylist.

Marianne Faithfull —
Singer/songwriter Marianne had her
first hit with a Stones-composed song.
She dated Mick, too, supposedly inspiring
"You Can't Always Get What You Want".

Tina Turner —
Tina joined Mick on stage during his US
Live Aid set in 1985 and the sparks flew
—turning it into the most talked-about
performance of the night.